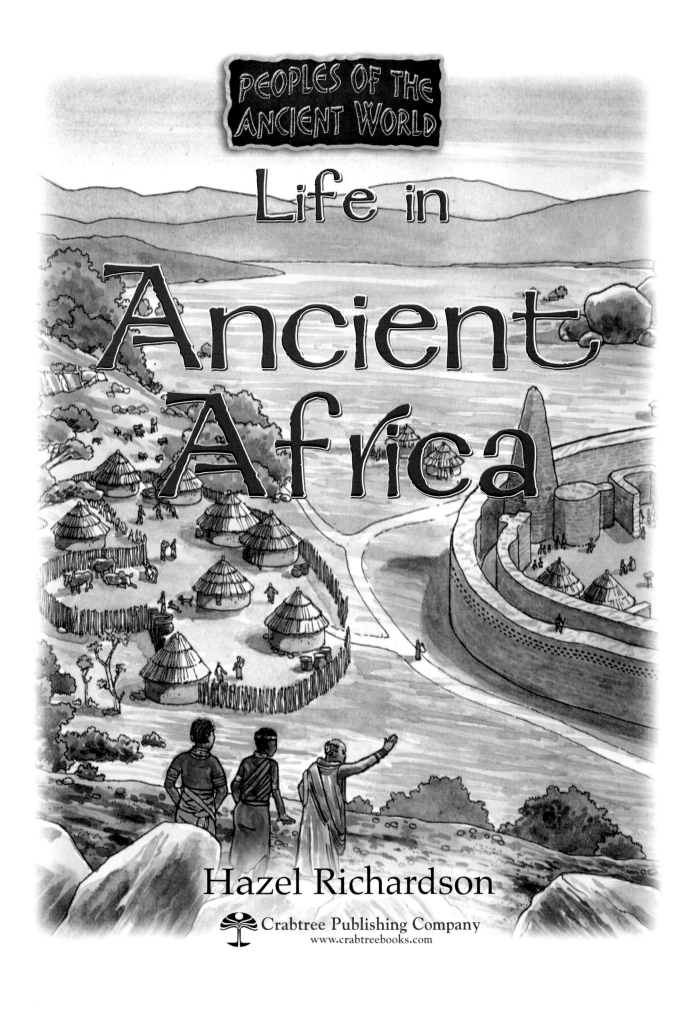

PEOPLES OF THE ANCIENT WORLD

Life in

Ancient Africa

Hazel Richardson

Crabtree Publishing Company
www.crabtreebooks.com

Crabtree Publishing Company
www.crabtreebooks.com

For Eben, Oliver, and Thomas

Coordinating editor: Ellen Rodger
Editors: Rachel Eagen, Carrie Gleason, Adrianna Morganelli
Production coordinator: Rosie Gowsell
Production assistance: Samara Parent
Scanning technician: Arlene Arch-Wilson
Photo research: Allison Napier
Art director: Rob MacGregor

Project Managment:
International Book Productions, Inc.:
Barbara Hopkinson
J. David Ellis
Sheila Hall
Dietmar Kokemohr
Judy Phillips
Janice Zawerbny

Consultant: Stephen Rockel, Ph.D, Department of History,
University of Toronto

Photographs: Archivo Inconografico S.A./Corbis: p.12; Art Archive/Antenna Gallery Dakar Senegal/Dagli Orti: p.24 (top); Art Archive/Bardo Museum Tunis/Dagli Orti: p.28; Art Archive/Biblioteca Nazionale Marciana Venice/Dagli Orti: p.31 (top); Art Archive/Egyptian Museum Cairo/Dagli Orti: p.3, p.9 (top); Art Archive/Museum of Carthage/Dagli Orti: p.17; Bildarchiv Preussischer Kulturbesitz/Art Resource, NY: p.24 (bottom); The British Museum/Heritage Images: p.20 (bottom), p.22 (top); Courtesy Charles Caulkin: p.16 (top); Egyptian National Museum, Cairo/Bridgeman Art Library: p.16 (bottom); David Else/Lonely Planet Images: p.10 (bottom), p.30; Jim Erickson/Corbis: p.18; Werner Forman/Art Resource, NY: p.11, p.14 (bottom); Owen Franken/Corbis: p.7; Anthony Ham/Lonely Planet Images: pp.4–5; Lindsay Hebberd/Corbis: p.25 (top); HIP/Scala/Art Resource, NY: p.13 (top); Courtesy of the Mapungubwe Museum, University of Pretoria: p.25 (bottom); Gideon Mendel/Corbis: p. 23; Christine Osborne/Corbis: cover, p.29 (top); Private Collection/Bridgeman Art Library: p.10 (top); Royalty Free/Corbis: p.20 (top); Private Collection/ Heini Schneebeli/Bridgeman Art Library: p.19 (top); Carmen Redondo/ Corbis: p.31 (bottom); Thelma Saunders/Eye Ubiquitous/ Corbis: p.21; Stapleton Collection/Bridgeman Art Library: p.9 (bottom); Patrick Ben Luke Syder/Lonely Planet Images: p.14 (top); Nik Wheeler/Corbis: p.13 (bottom)

Illustrations: William Band: borders, pp.4–5 (timeline), p.6 (map of Africa), p.8, p.15 (top), p.22 (bottom), pp.26–27, p.29 (bone)

Cover: A Gambian wooden mask with decorative cowrie shells.

Contents: Ancient art depicting Egyptian prisoners including a tattooed Libyan, a Nubian, and a Syrian prince.

Title page: A section of the enclosure, Great Zimbabwe.

Crabtree Publishing Company

www.crabtreebooks.com   1-800-387-7650

Cataloging-in-Publication Data
  Richardson, Hazel.
  Life in Ancient Africa / written by Hazel Richardson.
    p. cm. -- (Peoples of the ancient world)
  Includes index.
  ISBN-13: 978-0-7787-2043-0 (RLB)
  ISBN-10: 0-7787-2043-8 (RLB)
  ISBN-13: 978-0-7787-2073-7 (pbk)
  ISBN-10: 0-7787-2073-X (pbk)
  1. Africa--History--To 1498--Juvenile literature. I. Title. II. Series.
  DT24.R53 2005
  960'.1--dc22

            2005001099
            LC

**Published in
the United States**
PMB 16A
350 Fifth Ave.
Suite 3308
New York, NY
10118

**Published
in Canada**
616 Welland Ave.
St. Catharines
Ontario, Canada
L2M 5V6

**Published in the
United Kingdom**
73 Lime Walk
Headington
Oxford
OX3 7AD
United Kingdom

**Published
in Australia**
386 Mt. Alexander Rd.
Ascot Vale (Melbourne)
V1C 3032

Contents

Our Ancient Home

Africa is one of the most important places in human history. It is the birthplace of the earliest humans, and home to some of the world's oldest and most powerful civilizations. The histories of Africa's great empires and cultures are only just beginning to be understood.

The Earliest Civilizations

Ancient Egypt, one of Africa's earliest civilizations, arose about 4000 B.C. At the same time, the Nubian civilization, which came to **rival** ancient Egypt, was developing directly to the south. Many African civilizations emerged all over the continent, including the Aksumites, cultures from the Niger River Valley and the Swahili Coast, ancient Zimbabwe, and the empires of Benin, Ghana, Mali, and Songhai. Many great African civilizations traded with each other and with people from lands as far away as India and China. The ancient Africans built great cities, many villages, and cultural monuments, but they also became skilled farmers and **pastoral** herders.

Nile River is used for trade by Nubians and Egyptians
4000 B.C.

Ships sailed the Nile for trade for thousands of years.

Nubian civilization develops
2500 B.C.

The Nubian city of Kerma was a busy trade center.

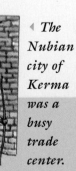

Aksumites settle near the Red Sea
500 B.C.

Large carved pillars were built by the Aksumites and placed over the tombs of their rulers.

Nok culture arises
300 B.C.

The Nok were skilled sculptors and potters.

What is a "civilization"?

Most historians agree that a civilization is a group of people that shares common languages or forms of communication, advanced technology, science, and systems of government and religion.

◀ *For more than 600 years, members of the Nubian royal family were buried inside the pyramids at Meroë after their deaths. The pyramids were made from red sandstone.*

Swahili culture arises along the eastern coast of Africa 100 A.D.

Spread of religion of Islam in Africa 700 A.D.

▼ *Many mosques were built in ancient Africa.*

Mali Empire expands 1235 A.D.

Great Zimbabwe built by ancestors of the Shona people 1250 A.D.

▼ *The stone walls of the great enclosure, Great Zimbabwe.*

Europeans begin to colonize Africa 1500 A.D.

The African Lands

Africa is a continent that lies half above the equator and half below it. This gave ancient Africa a warm and varied climate and landscape. The north was covered by arid desert, while dense rain forests and swamps stretched across humid central Africa. Lush grasslands lay in the temperate south.

The Nile Valley

The longest river in ancient Africa was the Nile. The ancient civilizations of Egypt and Nubia developed along this river, which flooded each summer after heavy rains and covered the river plains with silt. Eyptians and Nubians grew crops in the rich soil and built **irrigation** canals to bring water from the river to the fields. The river plains were surrounded by tropical grasslands, or savannas, which the Egyptians used to herd cattle and hunt animals for food and for their horns, tusks, and skins.

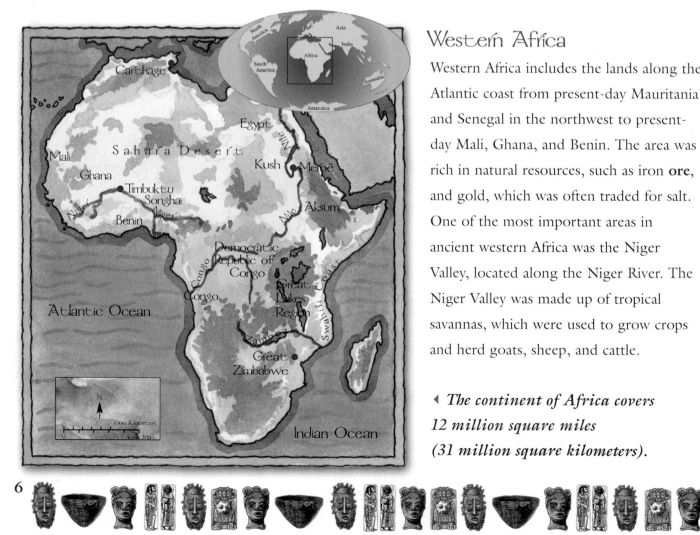

Western Africa

Western Africa includes the lands along the Atlantic coast from present-day Mauritania and Senegal in the northwest to present-day Mali, Ghana, and Benin. The area was rich in natural resources, such as iron **ore**, and gold, which was often traded for salt. One of the most important areas in ancient western Africa was the Niger Valley, located along the Niger River. The Niger Valley was made up of tropical savannas, which were used to grow crops and herd goats, sheep, and cattle.

◀ *The continent of Africa covers 12 million square miles (31 million square kilometers).*

Central Africa

Central Africa, which includes the present-day Congo and Democratic Republic of the Congo, straddled the equator. The weather was warm and humid year-round, with rain almost every day. The peoples of ancient central Africa hunted animals and gathered fruits and edible plants. They also fished in forest streams and lakes. There were five large lakes in this area, which is now called the Great Lakes region. Besides fishing, people in this region farmed and raised livestock, especially cattle and goats.

The Eastern Highlands

The lands of eastern Africa faced the Red Sea and the Indian Ocean and were rich fishing grounds. The mountains provided **granite** to build houses, temples, and monuments. There were also rich deposits of gold and copper to make tools, jewelry, and many other decorative items. The land received enough rainfall to grow two lots of crops each year, including the grains teff, sorghum, and millet.

Southern Africa

Southern Africa was an area of savanna and desert. The civilization that built Great Zimbabwe arose in the savannas near the Zambezi River, the fourth largest river system in Africa. The land was rich with gold, iron, and copper mined to make jewelry and tools. Antelope and rhinoceros were hunted for their skins and horns. The climate was temperate, and farmers grew sorghum and millet.

The Sahara and the Sahel

The Sahara is the largest desert in the world. Before a change in climate made it into a desert, the area was covered in savannas, rivers, and lakes. As the Sahara began to expand, the people who lived there moved south to the Sahel, a region on the southern edge of the Sahara Desert that stretches from northern Senegal and Mauritania right across to Mali, Burkina Faso, Niger, Chad, and into the Sudan. The Sahel lands were rich in gold and salt. Trading these two goods brought much wealth to the Sahel peoples.

▲ *The Sahara Desert continues to expand by half a mile (0.8 kilometers) each month.*

Empires of Africa

Many cultures co-existed in ancient Africa. The Nubians, Aksumites, and the peoples of Great Zimbabwe and the western African civilizations developed wealthy trading societies ruled by kings or pharaohs. Some societies did not have a ruler, but were organized by family groups, or clans.

Kings and Clans

Ancient African cultures were led by the most powerful and wealthy people, who were the kings, queens, pharaohs, and nobles. They controlled land and trade. Some ancient African societies were led by a village elder, priest, or the head of a powerful clan. Sometimes the most important person was the person who owned the most cattle.

Farming and Herding

Many ancient African cultures were farming or pastoral societies. Cattle were herded as domestic livestock in the central Saharan highlands as far back as 5000 B.C. In farming cultures, each person had a role in making sure that there was enough food to eat. Men fished, farmed, or herded animals, moving them around the countryside to take advantage of green pastures. Women were farmers who also looked after their children, worked in the fields, and prepared food. Many ancient African societies kept slaves who were often war captives from other cultures. Slaves usually had no choice in what work they did but some slaves achieved positions of power. Slaves were traded among other cultures and some even served as soldiers in ancient armies.

▲ *A trader from ancient North Africa.*

◄ *Slaves were taken in wars and raids and were often traded.*

Ancient Egypt

The ancient Egyptian civilization developed along the banks of the Nile River between 4000 B.C. and 3500 B.C. Over the next 3,000 years, it became one of the world's richest and most powerful civilizations. Enormous stone pyramids were built throughout ancient Egypt as tombs for the powerful Egyptian rulers, or pharaohs. Egyptian armies invaded and conquered many countries, including the land of the Nubians to the south, ancient Israel, and ancient Syria. Ancient Egyptian civilization ended in 30 B.C., when the **Roman Empire** defeated Egypt's last ruler, Cleopatra.

▲ *Libyan, Nubian, and Syrian prisoners who were captured by the Egyptians are shown on this ancient plaque.*

The Nubian Kingdoms

To the south of ancient Egypt lay the land of the Nubian people. The Egyptians called this land Kush. The Nubians developed a great civilization that lasted from 2500 B.C. until 300 A.D. Egypt invaded Kush in 1550 B.C. and ruled the Nubians for 450 years. After Egyptian rule ended, the Nubians began to build up their armies and wealth. By 757 B.C., they were so strong that they invaded and conquered Egypt. For the next 100 years, Nubians ruled Egypt. After the Nubians were forced out of Egypt, they moved their capital city to Meroë. There, the Nubians lived peacefully, trading with Egypt and Greece, until Meroë was destroyed in 300 A.D. by Aksumite invaders from the east.

◀ *The Nubians adopted Egyptian clothing styles.*

The Aksumites

Around 500 B.C., a group of people **migrated** from Arabia across the Red Sea to Africa. The migrants intermarried with people already living there. These people eventually became the Aksumite civilization. The Aksumites produced goods such as pottery and worked metal into objects they could use. They were a great trading nation, exporting goods, such as ivory and emeralds, and importing jewelry, fabrics, and wine and other items from India, Egypt, Greece, and Rome. Aksum began to decline around 600 A.D. when **Arab** traders took control of the Red Sea trade routes between Africa, Arabia, and India. Unable to trade, Aksum lost much of its wealth and the empire fell apart.

▲ *A brass mask of the Soninke people of ancient Ghana. The mask was used in ceremonies.*

Ancient Ghana

In 600 A.D., in an area of western Africa between present-day Mauritania and Mali, the empire of Ghana developed into one of the most powerful African kingdoms. Led by the Soninke people, ancient Ghana expanded its land and wealth by conquering many neighboring peoples with its strong army. The capital city was made up of two towns. The king and his nobles lived in one, while the merchants lived in the other. Most of the other people lived with their families in large farming communities. The Soninke were great traders who used camel caravans to transport goods, such as salt and gold. Around 1075, neighboring Berbers, a people from northwestern Africa, attacked Ghana after the Soninke conquered one of their trade centers. The Berbers were united under a **Muslim** dynasty called the Almoravid dynasty. Many of the Soninke people moved south to escape Almoravid attacks. The trade routes changed to follow the people, and the empire of Ghana eventually declined.

◄ *The Aksumites carved many large stelae, or granite pillars, and placed them over royal tombs. About 119 of these stelae still exist, including these in what is now Ethiopia.*

The Kingdom of Mali

The Mali civilization was developed by the Mandinke people, who controlled the land south of the kingdom of Ghana. Between 1230 and 1430, the Mandinke people took over surrounding communities, eventually developing a large civilization called the kingdom of Mali. Mali controlled the empire of Ghana's old territory and surrounding land, in what are now in the present-day countries of Senegal, Mauritania, Guinea, and Mali. The Mali people controlled almost all the gold trade through the Sahel area of Africa and in doing so became very wealthy.

The Songhai Empire

The Songhai kingdom, in what is today northwest Nigeria and western Sudan, began around 800 A.D. The Songhai kingdom became the largest empire in Africa, with several thousand cultures under its control. The city of Songhai was part of Mali in 1430. After the ruler of Songhai drove out invading Berbers from around his city, he created a new empire. The Songhai empire grew very large over the next 180 years. It collapsed in 1612.

Benin

In the forests of western Africa, people lived in small villages ruled by chiefs. Between 1000 and 1500, some of the village chiefs made **alliances** with each other and formed states. The largest state was Benin, in what is now southern Nigeria. Its capital was Edo, now Benin City. Benin rulers and nobles lived in the cities. They wore brass medallions to show their ranks. Most people in ancient Benin lived on small farms surrounding the cities.

Ancient Zimbabwe

Ancestors of the Bantu-speaking people, today known as the Shona, settled on the Zimbabwe Plateau around 200 A.D. They herded cattle, farmed, and mined gold and other metals. Using granite from the plateau, they built many cities, including a religious and political center that became known as Great Zimbabwe. This city, which was home to about 18,000 people, featured a hilltop palace and a high stone walled enclosure.

▲ *A stone carving of an Edo chief and his attendants from the palace walls in Benin City.*

▲ *(top) Rulers in ancient Benin wore brass medallions.*

Rulers and Warriors

Some parts of ancient Africa were ruled by kings and queens. They inherited the throne by being born into the royal family. Local chiefs and members of the ruler's family made up the government and helped the ruler make laws, collect taxes, and control trade.

Pharaohs of Egypt

The ruler, or king, in ancient Egypt was called a pharaoh. The ancient Egyptians believed that each pharaoh was a god who had descended from the sun god Amun-Ra. Each pharaoh had an enormous tomb or pyramid built for him. After he died, his body was mummified to prevent decay, then wrapped in bandages and placed in a decorated coffin called a sarcophagus.

Nubian Pharaohs

The Nubians ruled Egypt for almost 100 years, between 757 B.C. and 663 B.C. After the Nubians left Egypt, their kings continued to act like pharaohs but, unlike in Egypt, many of the rulers were women. The ruler was chosen from the royal family, usually by the mother of the king or queen. The most famous Nubian female pharaoh was Amanirenas, who led her army against invaders from Rome, a civilization that arose in what is today Italy. Amanirenas lost an eye in battle but still fought to victory.

Aksumite King of Kings

The Aksumite people called their king *negusa nagast*, which means "king of kings." Aksumite kings were strong rulers who expanded the kingdom and its trade routes. The Aksumites traded with the ancient Greeks. King Zoskales was a strong Aksumite ruler who was often described in ancient Greek writings as a king who boldly demanded trade treaties, or agreements, with ancient Rome and India.

▲ *The pharaohs of Kush wore a crown with a double cobra on the front to show that they controlled both Egypt and Nubia.*

Ghana's Warrior Kings

Ancient Ghana had a supreme ruler, known as the ghana, or "warrior king." The king became very wealthy by charging traders a tax, payable in gold, on the goods that traveled through his land. A huge army enforced the king's rule. In ancient Ghana, kingship passed through the female side of the family. The throne was inherited by the son of the old king's sister.

Mali's Mansas

The kings of ancient Mali were called Mansa, an Arabic word meaning sultan, or king. Mali's most famous Mansa was Sundiata, the Lion King. During his reign, Sundiata conquered neighboring territories, built libraries and universities, and introduced cotton growing and weaving to his nation.

Songhai Generals

Sonni Ali Ber, the first Songhai king, was famous for expanding the Mali territory of Songhai into a strong empire. His army captured the Mali city-state of Timbuktu, an important trading post and learning center. Sonni Ali Ber was not a popular ruler because he did not think education was important. After his death in 1492, the new king appointed scholars from Timbuktu to the government and made learning important to the Songhai people.

◀ *Mansa Musa, a wealthy and generous Mali ruler, was depicted on a European map from 1375 that showed his territory.*

▼ *Timbuktu, in present-day Mali, was a Muslim center of learning with prominent schools and libraries.*

Home and Hearth

Life for many ancient Africans was based on farming, fishing, herding, hunting, and later, trading. Many African families lived together in circular groups of houses, called compounds.

The Nubians

Most ancient Nubians lived in the countryside in round houses. These houses were built from wood posts covered with mud, with cone-shaped roofs made with grass. Nubian men wore short skirts or **loincloths** made from cheetah or gazelle skins. Women wore leather or linen skirts, and kept their upper bodies uncovered. Most people ate bread or a porridge made from grains they farmed, such as barley. Nobles could afford to eat roasted fish, beef, and wild foods, such as antelope and gazelle. They also ate vegetables and fruit, including lentils, chickpeas, dates, and figs.

▲ *People from many ancient African cultures lived in thatched-roof houses made from mud and often cow dung. The houses were cool in summer and warm in winter.*

▶ *Aksumite houses were round, with a cone-shaped thatched roof and a central fire pit.*

The Aksumites

Most houses in ancient Aksum were built by covering stone or wood with mud. In wealthy homes, clay pipes carried warm air from an oven below the floor to heat the rooms. Peasants and slaves wore simple leather clothing, while the wealthy wore cotton or sometimes silk cloth that was draped around the body. A common meal for Aksumites was a spicy stew made from beef, lentils, peas, and hot pepper. They also ate pancakes made from a cereal grain called teff.

Ancient Ghana

Peasant houses in ancient Ghana were made of mud bricks or wood and had only one room. In the cities, houses were larger and built of mud bricks. Ancient books describe the home of Ghana's king as surrounded by a large enclosure, like a city wall. The king and his government ministers wore clothing of fine cotton while most ancient Ghanians wore rough-hewn cotton garments. The king also wore his hair plaited with gold. Traders, made wealthy by Ghana's gold trade, wore clothing made from linen cloth imported from Egypt and Greece. The main crops grown in the area included millet, cotton, and sorghum, a plant similar to corn.

Ancient Mali

In ancient Mali, peasants lived in villages made up of small circular compounds, which were each surrounded by a wall. Members of related families lived within each compound. Men herded goats and sheep and grew millet and rice. Women made meals of boiled rice, bread made from millet, and fish or lamb stew. They also cooked, cleaned, cared for the children, and worked in the fields.

Pastoralists

Archaeologists and **anthropologists** are still slowly piecing together bits of history that explain how many farming and herding cultures lived in ancient Africa. Both nomadic and semi-nomadic cattle herders lived on the grasslands throughout Africa. Some built permanent settlements of mud houses with nearby cattle enclosures. Over time, cattle became very important to many ancient African cultures, so much so that owning several cattle was considered a sign of wealth.

Women of Ancient Africa

Women's roles within the family and society differed throughout ancient Africa. In most cultures, women were the primary caregivers for children and the elderly. Women also kept their families fed by working in the fields, milking cows, harvesting crops, winnowing grain, and also by preparing meals. Other women worked as potters, traders, weavers, and dyers. Life for most women was very difficult. Many women were slaves. Some women of wealth, royalty, and privilege were educated. In some cultures, women were priestesses who cared for shrines and temples, performed rituals to communicate with the gods, and healed people using herbs. In ancient Egypt and Aksum, many women owned property. Nubian and Egyptian women could become rulers. Women in some areas of Africa could even become chiefs.

Salt and Gold

Ancient Africa was the world's richest source of gold and ivory. It also had many items other nations considered exotic, such as ebony, and leopard and zebra skins. Salt was also an important item for trade for many African civilizations. Merchants from Europe and Asia sailed to Africa to trade for these treasures.

Nubian Trade

Trade between Egypt and Nubia began as early as 4000 B.C. Nubian traders took precious stones and gold, stone for building, leather for making clothing and shoes, and dates for eating to Eygpt. In return, the Nubians received Egyptian linen, glass, and jewelry. Merchants from Babylonia, in present-day Iraq, the Indus River Valley, and ancient India sailed across the Red Sea to trade with the Nubians. They brought pottery, cotton cloth, perfume, wine, and glass to exchange for gold, ivory, and slaves.

▲ Before coins, ancient Africans bartered, or traded, for items they needed.

▶ An Egyptian carving made from Nubian gold and ebony.

Aksum Exports

The Aksumites set up extensive trade routes between Africa, India, and Arabia. The Aksumite seaport of Adulis on the Red Sea was busy with Greek, Roman, and Chinese ships. The foreign traders arrived with cotton, linen, and woolen cloth, gold and silver jewelry, bronze, tin, silver, and steel. These were exchanged for slaves, live monkeys and elephants, elephant tusks, rhinoceros horns, hippopotamus leather, tortoise shells, and **musk** from the civet cat for making perfume.

The First African Coins

The Aksumites were the first peoples to use coins as a form of money. Other civilizations used salt, gold dust, or iron bars as currency. The Aksumites made many different gold, silver, and bronze coins, and used them to pay for foreign goods.

Carthage

Around 800 B.C., traders from Phoenicia, in what is now Lebanon, **colonized** the coast of northern Africa. The Phoenicians were the greatest sea travelers and merchants of their time and they called their African trading center Carthage. By 600 B.C., Carthage was one of the world's biggest cities, with two ports and the largest marketplace in the Mediterranean. Carthage was destroyed by the Roman Empire after a series of three wars known as the Punic Wars. The wars ended in 146 B.C. when Rome broke through the city walls after a siege that lasted three years. The Romans burned the city to the ground and killed nearly all the inhabitants.

The Swahili Coast

The Swahili Coast is a 1,500-mile (2,400-kilometer) stretch of coastline along the present-day East African countries of Kenya and Tanzania. It was a central area of trade between Africa and other countries, including Europe, Asia, and the Middle East, starting around 100 A.D. These early coastal communities in eastern Africa were centers for farming, fishing, and iron working. Over time, as trade in gold, ivory, and slaves increased, a sea-trading economy was established. The Swahili Coast is named after the Swahili language spoken by the people in the region. Over time, this African language adopted many Arabic and Persian words and became the language of trade.

▲ *To make sure that Carthage was destroyed forever, the Romans sold all surviving inhabitants into slavery and spread salt over the farmland so that crops could no longer be grown there.*

Camel Caravans

Camels were first brought to northern Africa by Arab traders around 500 A.D. Two hundred years later, camels were transporting goods across the Sahara Desert. The camels could carry heavy loads and go up to nine days without water and weeks without food. Crossing the Sahara became less difficult, and trade with western Africa increased. Caravans of up to 1,000 camels, tied together from head to tail, made the journey across the Sahara sands from the Sahel to northern and eastern Africa in less than 40 days. Along the way, the caravans stopped at posts set up at **oases** for water and food. Over time, many of the desert oases became markets and meeting places for the caravan traders.

All the Sahel civilizations traded with the kingdoms of northern and northeastern Africa. They mainly traded salt and gold, but also slaves, pepper, ivory, **indigo**, leather, ostrich feathers, and beeswax. Caravans returning to Ghana, Mali, and Songhai from these areas brought back woven and decorated cloth, copper, and silver.

▲ *Camels can carry loads of up to 500 pounds (225 kg). The camel uses fat stored in its hump for energy. In ancient caravans, there was one camel driver for every six camels.*

Silent Trading

Silent trading was a type of trading practiced by Sahel civilizations. Merchants brought their goods to a spot on the riverbank, beat on a drum to announce their arrival, then left. Buying merchants came to examine the goods and laid down as much gold as they thought the goods were worth. The sellers returned to check the payment. If it was acceptable, they took the gold and left the goods. If it was not enough, they left both. The buyers returned and added more gold in payment, again beating a drum to alert the sellers. This continued until the sellers were satisfied or the buyers had reached the highest amount they were willing to pay.

Trade with Ancient Zimbabwe

Ancient Zimbabwe was the busiest and largest trading kingdom in ancient southern Africa. It traded with other African regions, including Katanga in present-day Congo. Traders from ancient Zimbabwe met with merchants from Arabia, South Asia, and India at the bustling port city of Sofala, in present-day Mozambique. They traded mostly copper jewelry, leather, and gold for porcelain, ceramics, glass beads, and cloth.

▲ *Copper jewelry was traded in ancient Africa.*

The Salt Trade

Salt was one of the most precious items of the ancient world. The Sahel civilizations gained great wealth by trading salt, which was used to preserve food. In the trading cities of western Africa, salt was worth its weight in gold. It was sold at markets in enormous chunks. The main salt mines were at Targhaza in the Sahara Desert. Salt was mined by slaves and prisoners, many of whom had to work in the salt mines until they died.

▶ *Ancient African traders were attracted to the Sahara region, where salt was plentiful.*

Worship and Beliefs

Most ancient Africans worshiped many gods, including a supreme creator god. They also believed in a life after death that was much like life on Earth. Over time, as they came into contact with peoples from other lands, some African civilizations came to accept the beliefs of other religions.

The Spirit World

Cultures throughout ancient Africa believed that every object, alive or not, contained a spirit. They also believed that the spirits of dead **ancestors** lived on Earth. Both these types of spirits could be angered or pleased by people's actions. Angry spirits were thought to cause bad luck. Religious leaders held ceremonies with singing and dancing to honor the spirits, and people offered food, drink, and other gifts to keep the spirits happy. Many African cultures still hold these beliefs today.

▶ *A stone sphinx stands outside the pyramid of Taharqa, the last Nubian ruler of Egypt.*

Nubian Burials

In Kerma, the first capital city of the Nubian kingdom of Kush, dead kings were buried in small chambers in the center of huge mounds of earth. Stone models of ships were put around the body in the belief that they would carry the king on the river to the afterlife. Influenced by the Egyptians, the Nubians began to preserve their dead rulers by mummifying them, starting around 900 B.C. They then placed the bodies in pyramids. Nubians who were not rulers were buried in pits. Food and the person's belongings, including pottery jars and tools, which were thought to be needed in the afterlife, were placed around the body. After the burial, the pits were covered with thousands of decorative black and white pebbles.

▲ *A carving of Bes, a god worshiped by both the Nubians and the Egyptians.*

Masks and Beliefs

Many ancient African civilizations honored the spirits of the dead. Communities held gatherings to watch dancers in masks that resembled their dead ancestors. People offered the dancers gifts of food in order to show their dead ancestors that they had not been forgotten. In ancient Nubia and Egypt, a mask resembling the dead person was placed over the face to help guide the spirit back to the person's body.

First Christian State

The early Aksumites worshiped several gods. Mahrem, protector of kings, was the Aksumites' supreme god. The Aksumites believed that three main gods controlled nature: Beher, the god of the sea; Meder, the goddess of the Earth; and Astar, the god of the heavens. Around 300 A.D., King Ezana of Aksum decided to make his land the world's first Christian state. Christianity was a religion that followed the teachings of Jesus Christ, who followers believed to be the son of God. By about 500 A.D., Christianity was the main religion of all Aksumites. It remained the major religion in what is now Ethiopia, even after the Aksumite civilization collapsed.

▼ *The Grand Mosque of Djenne in Mali is the largest mud brick building in the world.*

The Rise of Islam

Around 900 A.D., traders from Arabia spread the religion of Islam throughout northern and western Africa. Islam was founded by the prophet Muhammad, who was born in 570 A.D., in the Arabian city of Mecca. Muhammad received and spread the teachings of Allah, or God, and they were recorded in a holy book called the Qur'an. Followers of Islam are called Muslims. They believe that Allah is the only god, and that Muhammad was his prophet. Islam also spread through trade to the Swahili Coast in eastern Africa.

Words and Wisdom

Each of ancient Africa's thousands of cultures and civilizations developed its own spoken language or dialect**, and some had written** scripts**. A number of universities in the ancient world were located in Africa. Many students came from afar to study at them.**

Arabic Script

The most widely used script in ancient Africa was Arabic, the writing of the people who lived in Arabia, in what is now Saudi Arabia. Arabic spread through northern Africa and was adopted by the Sahel civilizations as they **converted** to Islam. At first, people spoke both their native language and Arabic. Eventually, Arabic script was used to write native languages.

Nubian Scripts

The Nubians in the kingdom of Kush developed a written language around 800 B.C. At first, they used Egyptian **hieroglyphs** to record their history and trade. After the Nubians moved their capital to Meroë, around 300 B.C., they developed their own written language. This was based on the ancient Egyptian script and had two forms: hieroglyphs and **cursive**. Hieroglyphs were inscribed on monuments. Cursive writing was simpler and was used for writing on papyrus. Archaeologists have decoded the sounds that the alphabet's symbols stood for, but they have not been able to translate the writing.

▲ *Ancient Nubian hieroglyphs recorded events. This one is from the Nubian city of Meroë.*

▼ *The symbols from the Aksumite language of Ge'ez were very similar to the Greek alphabet.*

Aksumite Scripts

The Aksumites had three main scripts, or forms of writing: Arabic, Greek, and Ge'ez. Ge'ez was a language created by the Aksumites, and was similar to Arabic. Ge'ez script developed around 300 A.D. At first, there were only symbols for consonants, but the script was soon changed so that each symbol showed a syllable of a consonant and a vowel. There were 33 letters in Ge'ez, which were written from left to right.

Bantu Speakers

As the Bantu-speaking peoples migrated from western Africa, their languages combined with that of the other African peoples to create new languages. All ancient Bantu languages were spoken only. In the 1700s, a written form of the language was developed. Today there are over 500 Bantu languages, spoken by 200 million people. The most common ones are Swahili, spoken on Africa's east coast, and Shona, spoken in Zimbabwe.

Watching, Listening, and Learning

Most ancient African children learned by watching adults carry out their work, by playing games, and by listening to stories. Children in all societies played a game called mancala to learn counting and mathematical skills. Children also learned by participating in initiation rituals, or knowledge ceremonies, in which they were taught about such things as their family and community history and their future roles as adult men and women. In western Africa, people also learned history by listening to the stories of griots. Griots were people who were specially trained to memorize and recite history.

Schools and Universities

The spread of Islam and Arabic writing through ancient Africa led to the founding of many schools and universities. One of the largest centers of learning was Timbuktu. By the 1100s, it had three universities and 180 schools. Students were taught the Arabic language and script by Islamic scholars, and memorized the Qur'an, the Muslim holy book. They also learned Islamic history, mathematics, astronomy, and sciences.

▶ *Mancala is an African game still played today that archaeologists think dates back to 1500 B.C. Game pieces are moved from one position, or pit, on the game board to another. Ancient Africans thought mancala tested intelligence.*

Art and Music

Ancient African art, jewelry, carvings, and paintings reflected the people's relationship to the land and animals, as well as their beliefs in gods who controlled the natural world. Music, dance, and storytelling were also an important part of daily life.

Nubian Art

The Nubians were the first civilization in the world to develop a large-scale iron **smelting** industry for producing metal goods, and much of their greatest artwork was made of iron. Nubian artisans also made priceless golden treasures, including the masks found in Egyptian pyramids and tombs.

Benin Bronze Art

The kingdom of Benin is best known for the large, lifelike brass and bronze heads made in honor of the kings. The heads, displayed in the palace, were usually images of the king, but sometimes were of members of the king's family. Bronze snakes decorated the royal palace in Benin and were a symbol of Osun, the god of nature. Benin artisans also made brass and bronze plaques for the palace that showed the history of Benin. The people of Benin considered the leopard the king of beasts and used it as a symbol of royal power in their art. Many bronze objects made for the king were of this wild cat.

Jewelry

Ancient Africans made most of their jewelry from gold. Nubians wore gold neck rings, arm bracelets, earplugs, and headbands. Attendants to the king of Ghana were described as having their hair braided with gold, while the king wore a golden cap, necklace, and bracelet.

▲ *The Nubian gold ring on the left shows the lion-headed god of royal power, Apedemak.*

▲ *The bronze heads of the Benin royal family were passed down from king to king.*

24

Ancient Zimbabwe Carvings

Animal imagery was common in the art of ancient Zimbabwe. Household items were decorated with simple carvings of many types of animals. The most famous pieces of art found in the city of Great Zimbabwe are bird sculptures carved from soapstone.

Music and Dance

Music was important to many aspects of ancient African life. It provided entertainment and accompanied games, contests, stories, and religious ceremonies. At festivals and special occasions, musicians played bone flutes and other instruments, while the other villagers played along with wooden drums and shakers, clapped their hands, and stomped their feet or danced. Royal courts kept their own musicians. Their instruments, including ivory trumpets, harps, and drums carved with the images of animals and gods, were seen as a sign of prestige.

African Folklore

Traditional beliefs and myths, many about birds, were passed down from generation to generation in ancient Africa through storytelling. Several birds, including hawks and eagles, were believed to be messengers of the gods. Many tales told of migrating birds bringing fertility with them. In others, birds were reincarnated, or reborn, humans. Taking eggs from a bird's nest was thought to bring bad luck.

▲ *The kora is an ancient 21-string harp from western Africa that is still played today.*

▼ *The rhinoceros was a symbol of power among the Shona people. This gold-plated rhinoceros is from Mapngubwe, an ancient Shona settlement in southern Africa.*

The Great Enclosure

The huge walled structure known as the great enclosure is the largest structure still standing in the ruins of the ancient city of Great Zimbabwe. The city was settled and grew over hundreds of years. At the city's height, around 1250, the enclosure is thought to have served as a religious center, a place where rulers and nobles lived, or a livestock enclosure.

1. The enclosure and city ruins are located on a mountain **plateau** in what is now Zimbabwe. Surrounding the great enclosure were wood and grass huts housing thousands of farmers and mine workers. The farmers raised and herded cows, which were the main food supply for the people, and grew grains and vegetables.

2. Cone-shaped towers in the enclosure are believed to have been used to store grain.

3. The walls of the great enclosure were built using stones cut from the granite on the plateau. The stones were laid without **mortar**. Some of these walls are 36 feet (10 meters) thick and 19 feet (5 meters) wide. The stones were laid so as to create gently curved walls that had a checkered pattern.

4. Steep stone paths led from the enclosure to terraces carved into the hills, to other stone buildings, including a structure that might have been a palace, and to mines in the surrounding hills.

5. In the hills, workers dug out ores. The ores were heated to high temperatures in furnaces. The heat would melt and separate the ores from the **minerals**, creating metals, such as copper and iron, that could be used to make tools, weapons, and jewelry.

African Legacy

In the last few decades, major discoveries have been made by archaeologists, which have helped us learn more about how ancient Africans lived and what they created. The science of archaeology is slow and expensive, so many archaeologists have only begun to unravel the clues from Africa's past.

Iron and Steel

In 1928, archaeologists discovered the remains of an ancient culture they had not known about before. They called it the Nok culture, after the Nigerian village where the remains were found. Little is known about the Nok people. What archaeologists do know is that they smelted iron to make arrowheads and tools. Most ancient cultures discovered copper and bronze before they discovered iron. The Nok moved straight from using stone tools to using iron ones.

The First Steel

Western African cultures began to produce steel from iron ore 2,000 years ago. The ability to make steel was the secret of African blacksmith castes, or groups, who were believed to possess magical knowledge. Europeans did not discover a reliable method of producing steel until the 1800s. Archaeologists believe that one of the oldest methods for making steel was invented by peoples living in what is today Tanzania. The way in which ancient steel was made is only now being discovered.

▲ *African traders unload iron ore from a boat and weigh it on scales in this Roman tile mosaic.*

◄ *Palm oil was used in ancient Africa to make palm oil wine, which is still a popular drink in Africa today.*

The First Mathematicians

Ancient Africans were skilled mathematicians, and archaeologists believe that they were the first people in the world to create calendars and make calculations. A baboon bone found near South Africa is the oldest mathematical object in the world. It is 33,000 years old, and has notches on it that represent numbers. The 23,000-year-old Ishango bone, found in Congo, has a calendar engraved on it, which is based on the cycles of the moon. The ancient Egyptians and Nubians developed a great deal of mathematical knowledge. Many famous Greek scholars, including Pythagoras, studied mathematics in Egypt. The ancient Nubians and Egyptians used this knowledge to develop important ideas, especially about geometry, that are still taught in schools today.

Important Oil

Ancient peoples in western Africa began farming the oil from palm trees around 5000 B.C. The palm tree had many uses. Its wood and branches were used for building and its leaves for weaving into mats and baskets. Ancient Africans learned how to extract palm oil from the red fruit of the oil palm. The fruit was mashed and boiled in a large pot. The liquid was poured through a sieve to remove the mashed fruit, leaving palm oil in the water. The oil and water mix was left to separate and the water poured off. Palm oil was used to fry food, and to make bread and candles. Most palm oil is still produced in western Africa today. It is a major ingredient in soaps, lotions, creams, and margarine.

◄ *Some archaeologists believe that the Ishango bone is a six-month calendar. Others think that it is an ancient calculator.*

Political Upheaval

Many ancient African civilizations declined because of attacks and invasions by other cultures. When European nations discovered the continent's rich natural resources, they invaded many African countries. Millions of Africans were enslaved, and Africa's resources were stolen.

End of the Empires

War and invasion were common in ancient Africa. Attacks and invasions disrupted trade routes. Without the wealth from trade, many civilizations could not support large armies to defend themselves. Some African civilizations, such as the Nubian kingdom of Kush, survived for thousands of years. Others lasted only a few hundred years. The arrival of European explorers led to the breakdown of the last of the African empires.

European Exploration

Portuguese explorers first sailed down the west coast of Africa in the 1300s. They were looking for a trade route to India and China. By the 1400s, they were exploring many of the lands south of the Sahara Desert. The Europeans were stunned by the rich gold deposits there. They set up trade routes through the African kingdoms to obtain this precious metal.

▲ *Modern Aksum is in Ethiopia.*

◀ The slave trade killed countless numbers of Africans and brought others to North and South America.

The Slave Trade

Portuguese traders brought copper, guns and ammunition, horses, and iron tools to trading towns along the African coast to trade for African gold. They quickly learned that African slaves were highly valued by Arab traders living in Africa. By 1450, the Portuguese were trading thousands of slaves at ports along the African coast. The slave trade grew after North and South America were colonized in the 1500s. European plantations in those colonies needed a labor force to clear ground, build, and work on sugar plantations. Over the next 300 years, more than ten million Africans were captured and shipped to these plantations as slaves.

Europeans Colonize Africa

From the 1500s through the 1800s, England, Germany, Portugal, Italy, France, and Holland seized most of Africa and divided it among themselves. The European colonizers often plundered Africa's natural resources and destroyed many African monuments and historical treasures in their search for gold and land for farms and plantations. Africans resisted enslavement and European colonization, sometimes quietly and sometimes through armed struggle. Many of these struggles, in which colonial governments and ways of life were toppled and replaced with African ones, continued until the late 1900s.

▶ *Italian soldiers took this ancient Aksumite pillar, or stelae, from Africa in 1938. Leaders in Ethiopia have asked for it to be returned.*

31

Glossary

alliance A partnership between people or countries

ancestor A person from whom one is descended

anthropologist A person who studies the way people lived in the past

Arab A group of people originally from the Arabian peninsula

archaeologist A person who studies the past by looking at buildings and artifacts

colony Distant territories belonging to or under the control of another nation

convert To change religion

cursive A style of writing in which all the letters of a word are joined together

dialect A version of a language that is used in one region

ebony A type of hard, dark wood

granite A type of hard rock used to make buildings and monuments

hieroglyph A picture or symbol used to represent the meaning or sound of words and letters

indigo A blue dye made from the indigo plant

irrigation The process of supplying water to dry land using ditches, streams, or pipes

ivory Hard material that makes up the tusks of animals, such as elephants

loincloth A piece of cloth worn around the waist, hips, and lower abdomen

migrate To move from one country or region to settle in another

minerals Naturally-occuring, non-living substances, such as diamonds or crystals

mortar A blend of sand, lime, water, and sometimes cement used to hold bricks and stones together

musk A substance with a strong odor produced by some animals that is used to make perfume

Muslim A person or people who follow the religion of Islam

oases Places in the desert that are fertile or green due to the presence of water

ore A rock that contains minerals, such as copper and iron, that are used to make metals

pastoral Relating to the country or country life

plateau An area of flat land that is higher than the land around it

rival A competitor

Roman Empire A group of territories under the control and rule of Rome

sandstone A type of rock that is formed by compacted sand

script Recorded language

smelt The process of removing a metal from an ore, usually by melting

temperate Weather, temperatures, or climates that are neither too hot nor too cold

winnow To separate the chaff, or shell, from a grain

Index

1 2 3 4 5 6 7 8 9 0 Printed in the U.S.A. **4 3 2 1 0 9 8 7 6 5**